My Special Girls

My Special Girls

Poems of Love Given & Lives Shared

Janie Emerson

Cover Photo by Janie Emerson

Copyright © 1999, 2025 Janie Emerson. All rights reserved. This book or any portion thereof may not be reproduced or used in any manner whatsoever without the express written permission of the publisher except for the use of brief quotations in a book review.

ISBN: 978-0-9716320-7-3
Cover photo by Janie Emerson
Book design by Janie Emerson
Printed in the United States of America.

JEM Enterprises
La Jolla, California

ShamrockWisdom.com

DEDICATED TO

My Special Girls,
Mollie and Gwennie,
who touched and
healed all with love and
inspired Shamrock Westies
who changed
lives forever.

CONTENTS

Introduction	ix

DREAMS

Simply Love	3
Special Spirit	5
My Best Friend	7-8
Doggie Dreams	9
Everyday	11-12
My Mollie & Me	13-14
Our Dreams	15-16
Together	17
Our Mom	19-20
Special Friends	21
Love Of My Life	23

PLAY

Coming Home	27
Sunshine Girl	29
Special People	31-32
Listening	33-34
Our Special Places	35
Pillow Toss	37
My Blue Angel	39

CONTENTS

To My Sister	41
Time Moves On	43-44
Furry Faces	45

LIFE

I Cry Alone	49
My Little Angel	51-52
Soul Mates	53-54
Love & Loss	55
Gentle Gwennie	57
I Can Fly	59-60
Forever More	61
Empty Spaces	63
The Pain	65-66
I Sleep Alone	67
We Are Whole	69

EPILOGUE

Love goes on….	73
About The Author	75

INTRODUCTION

My Mollie was my 1st dog and my 1st West Highland White Terrier (Westie). This special little 3 pound puppy weaseled her way into our lives and made each day a joy. Gwennie joined her a year later. Together they showed us how to live life and to play with abandon.

These 2 special beings opened our hearts and showed us how to live life….to enjoy every moment, to turn all into play, to love with abandon, and to be present in every moment.

Our special pets have so much to teach us. They "talk to us" all the time. Take time to be present with them, to listen to them, to learn from them as they teach us.

LISTEN - LEARN - LOVE

DREAMS

SIMPLY LOVE

You see it in
Their loving eyes,
The cock of a furry head.

You hear it in
Their happy sounds,
The yelps of total joy.

You feel it in
Their warm snuggles,
The licks you do receive.

They tell us in
Their wagging tail,
The glee upon their face.

They love us in
Ways we only feel,
And, it is simply love --

Special Spirit

I have a special spirit
Who lives inside of me.

I know this special spirit
For I can feel its' glee.

I trust my special spirit
For it is part of me.

I feel this special spirit
So happy and so free.

I love my special spirit
Who dwells inside of me.

My Best Friend

She lights up my world
    with joy and glee.
She gives me great love
    and a "joie de vivre."

My furry friend knows
    the real real me.
She reads my mind -
    helps me to be.

Her love is a bounty
    for all to behold.
It shines in her eyes
    each one she enfolds.

We walk side-by-side
    16 years of great joy.
We play catch, each day,
    with her favorite toy.

Her love is my life,
> true soulmates, one.
Starting each day with
> snuggles at dawn.

We are best of friends,
> my Mollie and me.
We spread love and joy
> to all that we see.

She spreads love and joy
> to all that she sees.
We are best of friends,
> my Mollie and me.

Doggie Dreams

Its warm and its cozy
    Snuggled in bed.
My body curled up
    See only my head.

I whimper and moan
    Asleep in my bed.
You wonder what it is
    Now in my head.

Its running and bounding
    Never in bed.
My body a quiver
    At what's ahead.

I shake and I paw
    Even in bed.
Its there I just know
    Not in my head.

Its warm and its safe
    Here in my bed.
In dreams I can catch
    What is in my head.

Everyday

Everyday is so precious with my
    "Girls".
We sit quietly in the garden
    and drink in each other.
We absorb the warmth of the sun
We enjoy each others love.

Life is precious
Love is pure.

These moments are special with
    my puppies.
We sit peacefully together
    and dream our dreams.
We are one in this moment
We bask in the warmth of our souls.

Love is pure
Life is precious.

The nights are a wonder with
      my "Girls".
We entwine our bodies
      and relax in our arms.
We cuddle together under the quilt
We merge and are one.

Life is precious --
          Everyday

My Mollie & Me

We sit together and
    share our dreams.
We walk along the sand.
She sits with me and
    we just know --
Our thoughts, not words
    so smoothly flow.

We trust and love
Our spirits merge.

We are companions
    stride for stride --
Sit together on the sand.
She looks at me
    with adoring eyes.
Our looks, not words
    reflect the love.

We are true soul-mates
Our spirits are one.

We share the warmth
    of souls as one.
We walk along the sand.
She stays with me
    for we are one,
My Mollie and me ...
    my special friend.

Our Dreams

I dream of things
      that could have been.
Of things and places
      we will wander in.

I gaze at stars
      and see their light.
The sun and moon
      all in my sight.

I see through mists
      upon our shore.
I sniff and gaze
      and drink in more.

I love our dreams
      as part of life.
They calm my world
      and ease all strife.

I give to Mom
        hopes and prayers
To ease her soul
        if I'm not there.

I dream our dreams
        to never part
Our dreams forever
        together in our hearts.

Together

Gwennie gives me
>gentle peace --

Mollie gives me
>total life --

Together we heal
>and give love --

Together we are whole.

Gwennie spreads
>sunshine and joy --

Mollie spreads
>vision and dreams --

Together we see
>and give life --

Together we are whole.

Our Mom

She's always there,
So loving and kind.
Whenever we need her,
She's gentle and kind.

We sit in our window
Just watching for her.
We race and we play,
So happy with her.

The beach is our playground,
So happy and free.
We all laugh and play,
Such fun and so free.

Our Mom is our friend,
We love her so much.
She give us such joy
And never too much.

Our Mom is so special,
So caring and kind.
She cuddles and loves us,
She is one of a kind.

Special Friends

They come along,
Once or twice -
Special friends
Who are so nice.

No rhyme nor reason,
Nor sex nor breed.
Just a friend -
Our friend indeed.

They come so close,
A part of us -
Special friends
For life a must.

No lines nor fences,
Nor mine nor yours.
Just a friend -
Our friend for sure.

They come along,
Once or twice -
Special friends
Are ours for life.

Love of My Life

You make my heart sing
With fun and laughter.

You make my mind play
With dreams forever after.

Your sparkly eyes,
Your wagging tail,
Your furry face,
All wreathed in love.

You make my days aglow
With joy and happiness.

You make my life so full
With love our souls caress.

PLAY

Coming Home

Smiling faces
Full of glee,
Waiting at home
Just to see me.

Wagging tails,
Yelps of joy,
Happy I'm home
Bringing a toy.

Running circles
Around and around,
Making it home
Where love is found.

Snuggling close
Full of love,
Warming our home
With bushels of love.

Sunshine Girl

She smiles,
She laughs,
She has such fun.

She trots,
She plays,
She loves to run.

She sniffs,
She dreams,
She sits as one.

She gives,
She loves,
She is MY sun....

Special People

We have our special people
    Who come to visit us.
    So many special people
Who share our lives with us.

Our Rita comes to play with us
    And some times cleans the house.
    And Sam lets us supervise
As he paints our house.

We draw in special people
    To help us grow and be.
    We teach our special people
To live their lives so free.

So many special people
      Touch our hearts with love.
      We are such lucky puppies
To have our ones to love.

We have our special people
      The ones we love alot.
      So many special people
In our hearts such special spots.

Listening

They speak to us
But are we listening --
    Or rushing through days
    With agendas bursting.

They smile at us
But do we see it --
    Or just pat their head
    With minds adrift.

They look after us
But are we aware --
    Or running around
    With no time to spare.

STOP - they say
It is time to play!

They patiently await us
For hours and days --
    Our furry friends
    In hopes to play.

They really know life
For us and for them --
    Our needs, their dreams
    In reality do blend.

They love us so much
For our hearts receive
    Our special companions
    In love to just be.

Our Special Places

We have our special places
Where our dreams are made.
These are our special places
With sunshine and with shade.

A place to go
We only know.
To be - to really be.

We have our special places
Outside with clear, fresh air.
These are our special places
With love and joy to share.

Our place to go
We truly know.
To see - to clearly see.

So many special places
The beach, the clifts, the park.
Of all our special places
The best is in our hearts.

Pillow Toss

She peeks between the pillows,
A little sparkly face.
Her button nose and happy eyes
Surrounded by white lace.

She tosses pillows in the air,
A little playful minx.
Her fuzzy head and joyful grin
Burrowed in the chinz.

She arranges pillows on our bed,
Our little furry friend.
Her wagging tail and eager face
Appear just now and then.

She rests between the pillows now,
A happy furry face.
Her body hidden and eyes now closed
She rests among the lace.

My Blue Angel

She soars
She climbs
She flies with glee.

She floats
She zooms
She flies to me.

See me Mom,
So happy to be
My puppy body
Now soaring and free.

Feel me Mom,
I give you joy.
A love so pure
It makes us both free.

She darts
She spins
She fills my heart.

She soars
She climbs
She's always with me.

To My Sister

I come at night
> When you're asleep
To heal and watch
> And bless your sleep.

I love you still
> So never fear
We lay together
> No nights of fear.

Our Mom is sad
> We love her so
To heal her heart
> We bless her now.

Our love is strong
> It brings us cheer
Know we never part
> For I am here.

Time Moves On

As age comes in,
We slow a pace,
We sleep some more
     and live with grace.

Our dreams shine true.
We see them clear.
We see less well
     and strain to hear.

As time moves on,
We think of times
We played and ran,
     with joy not whines.

As time moves on,
We age a bit.
We snuggle with love
     and lights dimly lit.

As age comes in,
We see our life.
We dream of chases,
    the fun, not strife.

Our thoughts remain.
We remember all so well.
We love our life,
    the dreams, the fun.

        And time moves on....

Furry Faces

Where is the human touch,
The hugs that make life for me ?
It is those happy faces
That greet with love just for me.

They see me coming in my car,
And race up to the door.
It is those furry faces
That greet me at my door.

How can you carry worries
Of life upon your back,
If you have those happy faces
That say, "Oh, Mom you're back" ?

They greet with love, yelps and hugs
And many a kiss of total glee.
It is those furry faces
That make my life for me.

LIFE

I Cry Alone

I cry alone.
    My Girls are gone.
    So quiet now
And not a sound.

I cry alone.
    Pain I only feel.
    So deep it is
And does not heal.

I cry alone.
    Love pulled inside.
    So closed I am
And want to hide.

I cry alone.
    Each day is cold.
    So lonely it is
No one to hold.

My Little Angel

I wake each day
    and hope to see
Your pixie face
    right next to me.

Your eyes so bright,
    and nose so cold,
My furry heater
    when all is cold.

I touch your place
    it's cold and bare.
I cry in silence
    no one is there.

You were my light,
    my spirit bold.
My special friend
    when all is told.

I wake at night
    and hope to feel,
Your warming breath
    even and real.

Your place is here,
    your blanket unfold.
My little angel
    your spirit I hold.

Soul Mates

She is part of me,
        My very core.
Her eyes see into mine,
        Into my core.

I hold her close to me,
        She warms my soul.
Her eyes so clear and bright,
        Reflect her soul.

For 16 years or more,
        She is my heart.
Her bounce and glee in life,
        Her joyful heart.

Now her form is gone.
        I am so cold.
I look in her favorite spots,
        Now all are cold.

Her eyes light up my life,
        My inner core.
For now our bodies part,
        But not our core.

We see each other now,
        And we are whole.
She stays a part of me,
        In my very soul.

Love & Loss

We loved each other
    my Mollie and I.
Our souls entwined
    will never die...

She loves me still,
    my little Girl.
Her form has changed
    no body to lie.

The loss is a pain,
    a deep, dark spot.
I wander alone
    and cry alot...

Our love remains
    for Mollie and I,
Entwined forever
    our souls are one.

Gentle Gwennie

Miss Gwennie is gone
    our gentle girl.
She laughed, she played,
    she hunted squirrels.

Her sparkly brown eyes
    and happy smile,
Lit up our world
    for many a mile.

Not one thing defeated
    our Gwennie girl.
An indominable trooper
    In our world.

Gentle Gwennie a dreamer
    loved the outdoors.
Now she soars in freedom
    over our shores.

I Can Fly

I see the birds
    I want to catch.
But they fly off
    They circle and pass.

Now they are mine
    To catch at last.
I reach and snatch
    Not like the past.

For I can fly
    On wind and air.
My body is gone
    I go everywhere.

I see the birds
    They circle the sky.
So free they are
    To soar and fly.

The birds are mine
      To grab at will.
Now is the time
      No standing still.

For I can fly
      Up in the sky.
I move with ease
Now I can fly --

Forever More

My step is heavy
    My shoulders sag.
My heart is weary,
    I stare, I sigh.

My friend is gone.
    No longer here.
No hugs, nor licks,
    I miss her cheer.

She loved and laughed,
    Lived with glee.
Her spirit so special,
    For all to see.

Her soul is here
    We feel its touch
A spirit so strong
    And loves so much.

She will be ours
    In every pore
We feel her love
    Now and forever more.

Empty Spaces

Each morning I awake
    The hole is still there.
No furry faces looking up
    At me with loving care.

My soul starts to ache
    It aches with dispair.
First Mollie killed and gone
    Now Gwennie is not there.

We prayed for total healing
    To play and have fun.
But time was cut too short
    For Gwennie to even run.

My pain is so deep
    It touches to my toes.
I love each so much
    I do hope they know.

Each morning I awake
    Hoping Gwennie is still here.
Only cold and empty spaces
    Not even my Doodle Bug Bear.

The Pain

The pain is deep
>   A void inside.
It sears my gut.
>   I try to hide.

We had such fun
>   Our last few days
We ran and played
>   And caught some rays.

I wake at night
>   But you're not there.
I reach to your spot
>   Your pillow is bare.

I love you so
>   The pain is real.
Each day so long
>   The night a slow reel.

You were my life,
> My light, my joy.
I walk and breathe
> A wind-up toy.

The pain so real
> It comes and goes.
I look the same
> So no one knows.

Life goes on and
> On and on.
Each day and night
> So gray and long.

Our love is pure
> So clear and strong.
It touches our hearts
> And goes on and on.

I Sleep Alone

I sleep alone now
    that you are gone -
I reach for you,
    and you're not there.

I feel so cold
    with you now gone -
There is no joy,
    nor fun nor cheer.

I dream our dreams,
    but all alone -
I look for love,
    and none is there.

It's not the same
    just here alone -
There is a vast void
    a hole so dear.

I sleep alone --

We Are Whole

Be gentle with
> yourself, Mom.
> We are with you.

Enjoy life and
> every moment.
> We play with you.

See joy in all
> you do, Mom.
> We are with you.

Feel peace it is
> within you.
> We sit with you.

Be happy for we
> are one, Mom.
> We are whole.

EPILOGUE

Love Goes On ....

> We are with you -
> Our love surrounds
> you with joy and life
> forever....
>
> Mollie & Gwennie

ABOUT THE AUTHOR

JANIE EMERSON

Janie Emerson was born and raised outside Philadelphia, on the Main Line, and in La Jolla, California. She is married to Bob. For more than 16 years, their special Girls (West Highland White Terriers - Westies), Mollie and Gwennie graced their lives with love.

She is the author of the successful *Appreciate Each Day, The Magic of Me, Guided By Animal Angels, & Walking With Angels.* Janie has written for newspapers and won national awards for her poetry. Her poems have been recorded and published.

The inspiration for Janie's writings comes from life. For these poems, they come from her Westies and their wisdom. Janie's work opens you to the love and life of her Special Girls. The intent is to empower and to enhance your life through these poems.

Janie is a respected consultant and acclaimed speaker. She has been an advocate for women owned businesses nationally, an active community leader, and a successful breeder of top Champion Westie's.

Janie is currently working on two new exciting projects.

www.ingramcontent.com/pod-product-compliance
Lightning Source LLC
Chambersburg PA
CBHW062113290426
44110CB00023B/2797